summy Piano solo Package

No. 501- Advanced

D1413790

Contents

Alfred Music
P.O. Box 10003
Van Nuys, CA 91410-0003
alfred.com

ISBN-10: 0-87487-656-7
ISBN-13: 978-0-87487-656-7

Preface

The broad selection of pieces in this collection invites the student to explore a variety of styles, moods and techniques. While the pieces are not limited to one grade level, most of those in this book are appropriate for students who have had four or more years of study.

Comments by Jane Knourek, in drawing attention to the structure of the music, not only facilitate learning but stimulate expressive performance because they further understanding of the musical material the composer has used.

SUMMY-BIRCHARD MUSIC

Lament

The lowered third and seventh degrees of the scale are the "blue" notes of blues style. Stress these notes a little as you play the song-like melody above the bass ostinato. The second section (beginning meas. 19), with its syncopated chromatic harmonies, is very like a jazz improvisation. The concluding section is like the first but thicker in texture, louder, and with more rhythmic motion.

GILBERT ALLEN

COPYRIGHT © 1959 BY SUMMY-BIRCHARD COMPANY

Etude

Think of the right hand in the first section of this piece as two or three voices singing together and remember that the top voice is not always the most important; bring out chromatic changes in inner voices. To simplify learning measures 17-21, block the first three eighths of each group and notice that the fourth eighth often leads chromatically to the next group. The left hand in this section also moves chromatically, first in 5ths, then in octaves.

Allegro

from *Recreations*
ALEXANDRE TANSMAN

9

Boogie Rock

Even if you didn't know the name of this piece, you would still recognize the characteristic style: blues-like melody, rhythmic figure used throughout as a bass ostinato, and simple I, IV, V7 harmonic progression. For authentic style, play the dotted eighths and sixteenths in triplet rhythm: should sound as though written.

After a short contrasting section (meas. 15-22), the melody of the first part is repeated in parallel 3rds.

from *Swingin' Technic*
RICHARD SHORES

Steady boogie beat (♩=126)

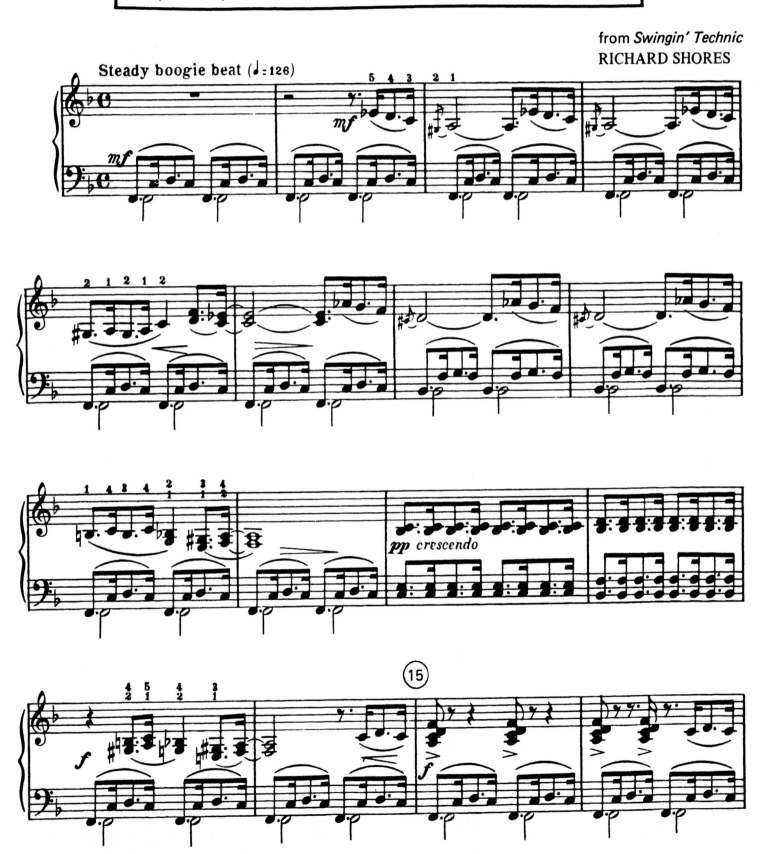

Chili Peppers

The rhythms in this piece are characteristic of Afro-Cuban music: eight notes grouped into 3 + 3 + 2 (♪♪♪ ♪♪♪), frequently contrasting with an even grouping of 4 + 4. In what way is the section beginning in measure 33 different from the beginning section?

Rumba tempo

OLIVE NELSON RUSSELL

Gallopade

Analyze this piece harmonically; it will be easier to learn if you know the chord progressions and the positions of the chords (root position? inversion?). Also analyze scale passages (chromatic or diatonic? form of minor?).

GENEVIEVE LAKE

To the Rising Sun

After a two-measure introduction, there is a quiet eight-measure melody in the left hand; this melody is repeated twice. What is added, or changed, in the repetitions to provide variety and contrast? What happens to the melody itself in the third repetition (beginning meas. 27)? Observe that there are only three different chords in the whole piece: I, V₇, and IV. Can you think of a good reason why the composer didn't use the second phrase of the melody in the concluding section?

TRYGVE TORJUSSEN   Op. 4, No. 1

Andante sostenuto

The Restless Sea

Don't let the sight of three staves bother you; the upper chords are the same as those on the first beat. In the middle section (meas. 9-32) tempo and meter changes and frequent modulations contribute, along with the rhythms, to the restless quality. The last part (beginning meas. 33) is like the first, with a few more notes filling in some chords.

Broadly, with feeling; not fast

BERENICE BENSON BENTLEY

Pinwheels

The right hand has F major scale passages up and down and around in the first section. Practice the right-hand broken chords of the second section (meas. 19-20, etc.) in blocked form until you are familiar with the harmonic changes. The harmony in measures 42-56 alternates between the tonic chord (F-A-C) and the diminished 7th on G♯ (G♯ - B♮ - D - F). After a repetition of the first section comes a last burst of fireworks.

WILLIAM L. GILLOCK

Presto

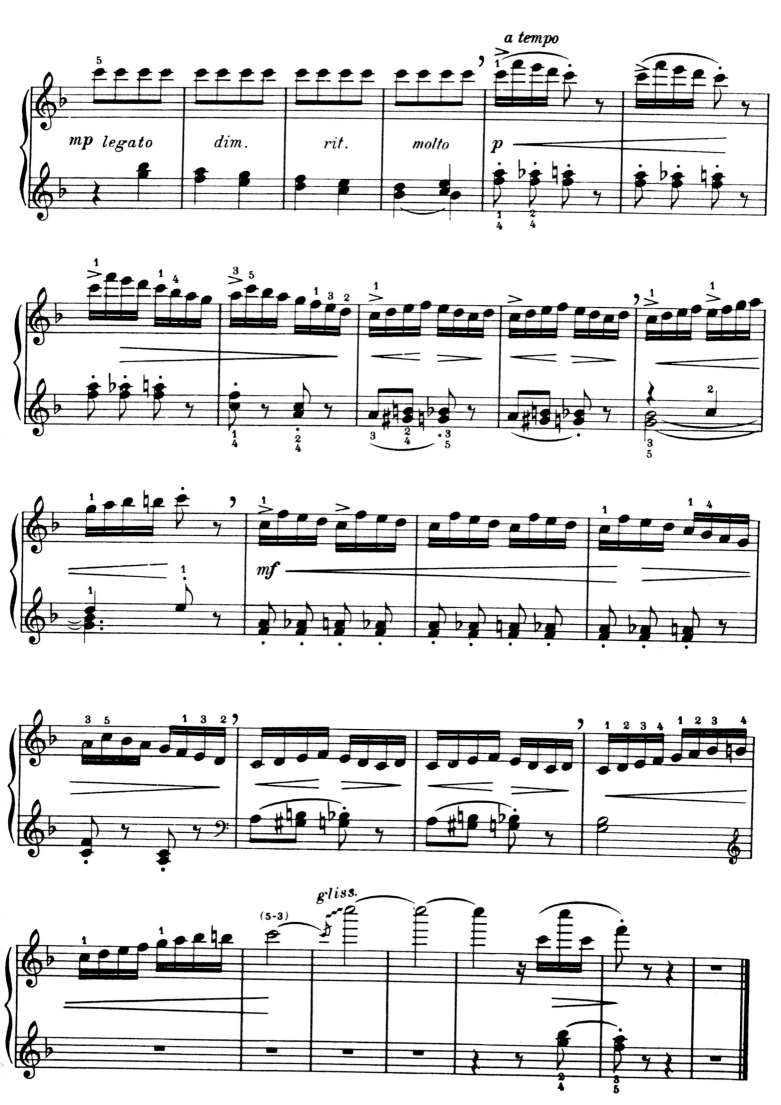

Mirage

Play the broken chords in blocked form and you will see that the first four measures are centered around the dominant 7th chord on E (E - G♯ - B - D). Measures 5-8 are similarly centered on the dominant 7th chord on C (C - E - G - B♭). The whole-step progressions in the right hand give the feeling of whole tone tonality at the outset. It is no surprise, then, to find the whole tone scale on C in measures 13 and 14. Notice in the broken-chord passages the frequent alternation of the major 3rds G♭ - B♭ and C - E, which are derived from the whole tone scale on C.

Flowing, but not fast (♩ = 80-92)

WILLIAM L. GILLOCK

COPYRIGHT © 1957 BY SUMMY-BIRCHARD COMPANY

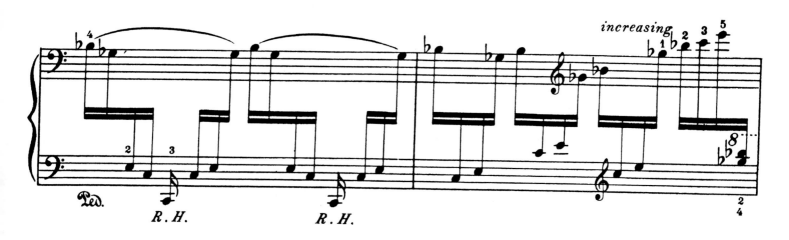

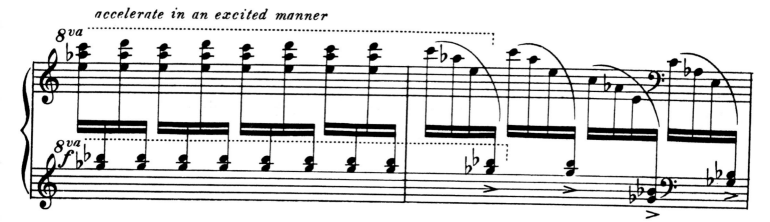

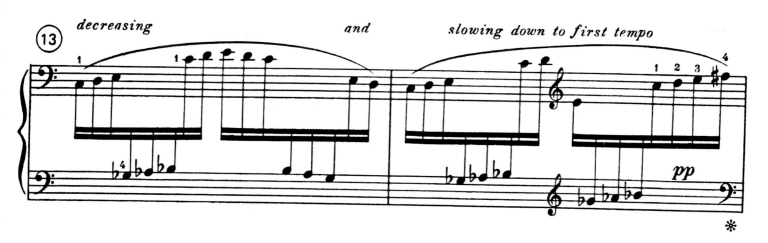

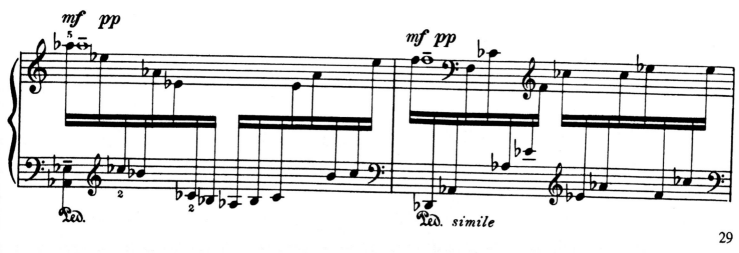

29